UNLOCKING SCRIPTURE

A GUIDE TO BIBLE VERSE MAPPING

TABLE OF CONTENTS

1. Introduction to Bible Verse Mapping
2. Why Bible Verse Mapping?
3. Getting Started with Bible Verse Mapping
4. The Verse Mapping Process
   - Step 1: Selecting a Verse
   - Step 2: Identifying Keywords
   - Step 3: Exploring Definitions
   - Step 4: Cross-Referencing
   - Step 5: Personal Application
5. Hands-On Example: Mapping Philippians 4:6
6. Creating Your Own Verse Map
7. Practical Tips and Tools
8. Sample Verse Maps
9. Reflective Questions and Exercises
10. Moving Forward: Developing a Verse Mapping Practice
11. Resources and Recommended Readings
12. Conclusion

CHAPTER 1

Overview: What Is Bible Verse Mapping?

Imagine having a tool that helps you uncover the deeper meaning of scripture, connects you personally to God's Word, and brings the Bible to life in new and exciting ways. That tool is Bible Verse Mapping.

Bible Verse Mapping is a visual, interactive approach to studying scripture. It involves breaking down a verse into smaller components—keywords, definitions, cross-references, and personal reflections—to uncover its full meaning and application. Rather than reading a verse quickly and moving on, this method encourages you to slow down, dig deeper, and savor every word. Think of it as creating a roadmap that guides you to a fuller understanding of God's truth.

The process is flexible and creative, incorporating tools like color-coding, diagrams, and notes to visually organize your study. Whether you're new to Bible study or a seasoned student, Bible Verse Mapping offers a fresh perspective that can transform your time in the Word.

PURPOSE: WHY BIBLE VERSE MAPPING?

The Bible is a living, breathing Word that speaks to us in every season of life. Yet, it's easy to skim over familiar verses or struggle to understand difficult passages. Bible Verse Mapping addresses these challenges by inviting you to engage with scripture in a deeper, more intentional way. Here's why it's so powerful:

1. Connect Personally with Scripture: Bible Verse Mapping encourages you to explore how each verse applies to your life. By reflecting on its meaning and relevance, you'll discover how God's Word speaks directly to your circumstances and spiritual journey.
2. Enhance Understanding: By breaking down verses into their components, you'll uncover nuances that might be missed in a quick reading. Understanding the original Hebrew or Greek meanings of keywords, the historical context, and related scriptures helps bring clarity and depth.
3. Make Study Engaging: Adding a visual element to Bible study can make it more interactive and enjoyable. Whether you're drawing connections between words, color-coding themes, or adding personal notes, the process engages your mind and heart in unique ways.
4. Develop a Habit of Reflection: This method encourages you to slow down and meditate on scripture, building a habit of thoughtful reflection that deepens your relationship with God.

Bible Verse Mapping is more than a study tool—it's an opportunity to let scripture shape your heart and guide your life.

This book is your guide to mastering the art of Bible Verse Mapping. Whether you're exploring scripture for the first time or looking for a new approach, you'll find step-by-step instructions, practical exercises, and real-world examples to support your journey.
Here's how to get the most out of this book:

HOW TO USE THIS BOOK

1. **Follow Along with Each Chapter:** Each chapter introduces a step in the Bible Verse Mapping process, complete with explanations and examples. Work through them in order to build a solid foundation for your study.
2. **Practice with Example Verses:** Throughout the book, you'll find example verses to practice mapping. These exercises will help you apply what you've learned and gain confidence in the process.
3. **Start Small and Build Gradually:** If you're new to Bible study or mapping, don't worry about tackling complex passages right away. Begin with short, familiar verses and gradually work your way up to longer or more challenging scriptures.
4. **Make It Your Own:** Bible Verse Mapping is a flexible process. Use this book as a guide, but feel free to adapt the method to suit your learning style and preferences. Experiment with different tools, layouts, and techniques until you find what works best for you.
5. **Reflect and Pray:** Each chapter includes reflection prompts to help you think about what you've learned. Take time to pray over the verses you study, asking God to reveal His truth and guide your understanding.
6. **Develop a Habit:** The more you practice Bible Verse Mapping, the more natural it will become. Aim to incorporate it into your daily or weekly study routine, allowing God's Word to shape your thoughts and actions over time.

A PERSONAL INVITATION

Studying scripture is one of the most rewarding investments you can make in your spiritual growth. Bible Verse Mapping is a tool that can help you unlock the richness of God's Word, understand His character, and strengthen your faith. As you move through this book, my prayer is that you'll not only gain new insights but also experience the joy and peace that come from spending time in God's presence.

Let's begin this journey together, one verse at a time. Open your heart, grab your Bible and notebook, and let's start mapping!

CHAPTER 2

WHY BIBLE VERSE MAPPING?

The Bible is a treasure trove of wisdom, guidance, and truth. Yet, even with the best intentions, it's easy to read quickly and miss the deeper layers of meaning woven into the text. Bible Verse Mapping offers a way to slow down, dig deeper, and truly engage with scripture. In this chapter, we'll explore why Bible Verse Mapping is such a powerful method for studying God's Word.

1. Deepens Understanding

Have you ever read a verse, felt its significance, but wondered if there was more to uncover? Bible Verse Mapping allows you to peel back the layers of a verse, revealing its richness and depth.

When we take time to examine individual words, explore their original meanings, and consider their context, we gain insights that might not be immediately apparent. For example, let's look at Psalm 46:10: "Be still, and know that I am God." On the surface, this verse offers a call for quiet reflection and trust. But when we dive deeper, we discover the Hebrew word for "be still" (raphah) can also mean "to let go" or "to surrender." Suddenly, the verse isn't just about quietness—it's an invitation to release control and trust in God's sovereignty.

Through Bible Verse Mapping, we can:
- **Understand original languages:** Hebrew, Greek, and Aramaic often carry nuanced meanings that enhance our understanding.
- **Uncover historical and cultural context:** Knowing the circumstances surrounding a verse adds clarity and relevance.
- **See connections across scripture:** Cross-referencing related verses reveals the unity of God's message throughout the Bible.

By taking a methodical approach, verse mapping opens up new dimensions of meaning, transforming how we understand and apply scripture.

2. Encourages Reflection

In today's fast-paced world, it's easy to rush through Bible study, ticking it off a to-do list without truly meditating on what we've read. Bible Verse Mapping encourages us to slow down and reflect.

Reflection is the heart of spiritual growth. When we take time to meditate on a verse, asking questions like, "What is God teaching me here?" or "How does this apply to my life?" we move beyond surface-level understanding. Verse mapping provides the structure to pause and consider:

- **What the verse says:** What is the message on a literal level?
- **What the verse means:** What is the deeper spiritual or symbolic meaning?
- **What the verse means to me:** How does this truth impact my life and faith journey?

Consider Philippians 4:13: "I can do all things through Christ who strengthens me." Without reflection, this verse might be interpreted as a promise of unlimited success. But mapping prompts us to reflect on its broader context—Paul's discussion of contentment in all circumstances. Suddenly, the verse isn't about achieving personal goals but relying on Christ's strength in every season, whether in abundance or need.

Bible Verse Mapping creates space for the Holy Spirit to work in our hearts, leading us to greater understanding and transformation.

3. Makes Study Engaging
Let's be honest: traditional Bible study can sometimes feel routine or overwhelming, especially if we don't know where to start. Bible Verse Mapping changes that by making study interactive and creative.

Using visual tools like color-coding, diagrams, and charts, verse mapping transforms scripture into a vibrant, engaging experience. Here's how:

- **Color-Coding:** Highlighting keywords, themes, or cross-references with different colors makes connections more visible.
- **Diagrams:** Drawing arrows between words, phrases, and definitions helps us see relationships within the verse.
- **Creative Freedom:** Adding personal notes, illustrations, or even artistic touches like doodles or stickers makes the process enjoyable and memorable.

For example, mapping Proverbs 3:5—"Trust in the Lord with all your heart, and lean not on your own understanding"—might involve highlighting "trust" in green (symbolizing growth), circling "heart," and drawing arrows to cross-references like Psalm 37:5 and Isaiah 26:3. This interactive approach keeps us engaged and excited to study.

When study feels fresh and dynamic, it's easier to stay motivated and consistent, turning Bible time into something we look forward to.

4. Strengthens Personal Connection

The Bible is not just a historical text; it's God's living Word, written for us. Bible Verse Mapping helps us experience scripture in a deeply personal way, strengthening our connection to God.

By breaking a verse down and reflecting on its meaning, we begin to see how God's Word applies to our unique lives and circumstances. The process invites us to hear His voice speaking directly to us through the text.

For example, consider Jeremiah 29:11: "'For I know the plans I have for you,' declares the Lord, 'plans to prosper you and not to harm you, plans to give you hope and a future.'" Mapping this verse might lead you to discover that it was originally written to the Israelites in exile—a promise of restoration after hardship. While its context is specific, its principles of God's faithfulness and hope for the future remain personal and relevant.

Bible Verse Mapping also fosters a sense of dialogue with God. As you reflect, you can pray over what you're learning, ask questions, and seek guidance for applying His Word. Over time, this practice deepens intimacy with God, making scripture study not just an intellectual exercise but a heartfelt conversation.

The Why Behind the Method

Bible Verse Mapping is more than a study tool; it's a way to engage with God's Word in a meaningful, transformative way. It deepens understanding by uncovering layers of meaning, encourages reflection by prompting us to meditate and apply scripture, makes study engaging through visual and creative methods, and strengthens our personal connection to God's Word. As you embark on this journey, remember that Bible Verse Mapping is not about perfection—it's about exploration, discovery, and connection. The ultimate goal is to draw closer to God and let His Word shape your heart and life.

Let's continue to the next chapter, where we'll explore the steps to get started with Bible Verse Mapping. Prepare to uncover the richness of scripture, one verse at a time!

CHAPTER 3

Getting Started with Bible Verse Mapping

Bible Verse Mapping is an exciting and creative way to deepen your understanding of scripture, but like any new endeavor, it helps to be prepared. In this chapter, we'll walk through the materials you'll need, tips for creating a conducive study space, and how to set up your very own verse mapping journal. Let's get started!

Materials Needed: The Bible Verse Mapping Checklist

Before you begin, gather the essential tools to make your verse mapping experience smooth and enjoyable. Here's a checklist of materials you'll need:

1. **A Bible**
   - Use any version you're comfortable with, but it's helpful to have access to multiple translations for comparison.
   - Consider a study Bible for additional context or footnotes.
2. **A Notebook or Journal**
   - Choose a sturdy notebook, binder, or journal specifically for verse mapping.
   - A blank or dot-grid journal works well for drawing diagrams and organizing your maps.

3. **Pens and Markers**
    - Use pens for writing notes and definitions.
    - Include markers or highlighters for color-coding keywords and themes.
4. **Bible Apps or Online Tools**
    - Apps like Blue Letter Bible, Bible Gateway, or Logos Bible Software are excellent for exploring original languages, cross-references, and commentaries.
    - Have a concordance or lexicon handy for deeper word studies.
5. **Optional Supplies**
    - Sticky notes for jotting quick ideas.
    - Washi tape or stickers for creative flair.
    - A ruler for drawing clean lines and boxes.

Having these materials ready ensures you can dive into your study without interruptions.

Setting Up Your Study Space

Bible Verse Mapping requires focus and reflection, so it's important to create a study space that fosters concentration and inspiration. Here are some tips for setting up the perfect environment:

1. **Find a Quiet Spot**
   - Choose a location where you can minimize distractions.
   - Whether it's a cozy corner in your home or a quiet spot in a library, make sure it's a place where you feel comfortable.
2. **Keep Your Materials Handy**
   - Organize your Bible, notebook, pens, and other supplies within arm's reach.
   - Use a basket, desk organizer, or dedicated shelf to store everything neatly.
3. **Make It Comfortable**
   - Use a comfortable chair and a well-lit workspace.
   - Add a candle, blanket, or favorite drink to make your space inviting.
4. **Set the Mood for Reflection**
   - Consider playing soft worship music or sitting by a window with natural light.
   - Pray before you begin to invite God's presence into your study time.

Your study space doesn't need to be elaborate; it just needs to be a place where you can focus and feel inspired to explore God's Word.

CREATING A VERSE MAPPING JOURNAL

A verse mapping journal is a central part of this process, giving you a dedicated space to record your insights, reflections, and creative maps. Here's how to set one up:

1. **Choose Your Journal Style**

   - Pre-Made Notebook: A standard notebook or journal with blank pages, lined pages, or a dot grid is ideal.
   - DIY Binder: Use a binder with loose-leaf paper or printable templates so you can rearrange or expand pages as needed.

2. **Organize Sections**

Divide your journal into sections to keep your study organized. Consider these categories:

   - Verse Maps: The largest section for recording your maps.
   - Study Resources: A space for definitions, cross-references, and notes from commentaries or sermons.
   - Reflections and Applications: A place to write how the verses apply to your life.
   - Prayer Journal: A section to jot down prayers inspired by your study.

3. **Set Up a Page Template**

Create a consistent format for each verse map to make your journal visually appealing and easy to follow. Here's a simple template:

- Top of the Page: Write the verse and its reference in your chosen Bible translation.
- Keyword Section: List and highlight significant words or phrases.
- Definitions Section: Record the original meanings and related insights.
- Cross-References Section: Note related verses and their references.
- Application Section: Reflect on what the verse means to you personally.
- Creative Area: Draw diagrams, add doodles, or include other visual elements.

4. **Add Creative Elements**
   - Use different colors to highlight themes or differentiate sections.
   - Add stickers, washi tape, or artistic designs to personalize your journal.
   - Include inspirational quotes or scripture at the start of each section to set the tone.

5. **Start Small**

Don't feel pressured to fill your journal immediately. Begin with one verse, and let your journal grow as you study.

A Personal Note

Your Bible Verse Mapping journal is more than a study tool—it's a record of your spiritual growth and encounters with God's Word. As you look back on completed maps, you'll see how God has spoken to you, taught you, and transformed your understanding.

Take time to set up your journal thoughtfully, knowing it will become a treasured resource in your faith journey. With your materials gathered, your study space prepared, and your journal ready, you're all set to begin exploring scripture like never before. In the next chapter, we'll dive into the step-by-step process of Bible Verse Mapping, starting with selecting a verse.

Let's continue this journey together!

CHAPTER 4

THE VERSE MAPPING PROCESS

Bible Verse Mapping is a simple yet powerful method to explore scripture deeply. In this chapter, we'll break down the process into five actionable steps. Each step builds on the previous one, guiding you through a rich and reflective study of God's Word.

Step 1: Selecting a Verse

The journey begins by choosing a verse that resonates with you. Your selection might come from a devotional, sermon, or personal reading.

Here are some tips for choosing the right verse:

- **Pick What Speaks to You:** Look for a verse that feels relevant to your current season of life or spiritual growth.
- **Focus on a Key Theme:** Choose a verse related to a topic you're studying, such as trust, forgiveness, or hope.

- **Start Small:** Begin with shorter verses that are easier to map. As you grow comfortable, move on to longer or more complex passages.
- **Pray for Guidance:** Ask the Holy Spirit to lead you to the verse God wants you to study.

Example Verse: Psalm 119:105 - "Your word is a lamp to my feet and a light to my path."

Practice Exercise:

Choose a verse that feels meaningful to you today. Write it down in your journal or notebook, along with its reference.

Step 2: Identifying Keywords

Once you've selected a verse, the next step is to identify its keywords. These are the words or phrases that carry the core message of the verse. Keywords are often:

- Action words (e.g., "trust," "walk," "seek").
- Nouns central to the verse (e.g., "lamp," "path," "heart").
- Repeated or emphasized terms.

Example:

In Psalm 119:105, the keywords might include "word," "lamp," "feet," "light," and "path." Each of these words contributes to the verse's imagery and meaning.

Practice Exercise:

 ake the verse you selected in Step 1 and underline or highlight the keywords that stand out to you. Write them in your journal and leave space to explore their meanings in the next step.

Step 3: Exploring Definitions

- To deepen your understanding, explore the original meanings of the keywords you've identified. Many Bible study tools, like a concordance or Bible app, provide definitions in the original Hebrew or Greek. Here's how to do it:
- Use a Bible Concordance or App: Look up the verse and find the keyword in its original language.
- Note the Definitions: Write down the root word, its definition, and any related insights.
- Consider Nuances: Pay attention to alternative meanings or cultural context that might add depth to the word's significance.
- Example:
    - For the word "lamp" in Psalm 119:105, the Hebrew word ner refers to a small oil lamp that provides just enough light to see the next step ahead. This insight emphasizes dependence on God for daily guidance.

Practice Exercise:
Look up the definitions of two keywords from your selected verse. Record their original meanings, definitions, and any additional insights in your journal.

Step 4: Cross-Referencing

Cross-referencing allows you to see how scripture connects across the Bible. It often clarifies or reinforces the message of the verse you're studying. Here's how to find related verses:
1. Use a Study Bible or App: Many Bibles include cross-references in the margins or footnotes.
2. Search by Keyword: Look for other verses that use the same keywords or address similar themes.
3. Compare Contexts: Consider how the cross-referenced verses expand or confirm the meaning of your main verse.

Example:
 For Psalm 119:105, related verses might include:
- Proverbs 6:23: "For the commandment is a lamp and the teaching a light…"
- John 8:12: "I am the light of the world. Whoever follows me will not walk in darkness…"

These verses highlight the continuity of God's guidance as light throughout scripture.

Practice Exercise:
Find at least two cross-references for your selected verse. Write them down in your journal and reflect on how they connect to your study.

Step 5: Personal Application

The final and most important step is to reflect on how the verse applies to your life. This step moves scripture from knowledge to transformation. Ask yourself questions like:
- What is God teaching me through this verse?
- How does this verse encourage, challenge, or guide me?

- What steps can I take to apply this truth in my life today?

Example:

For Psalm 119:105, you might reflect:

"This verse reminds me to rely on God's Word daily for guidance, trusting Him even when I can't see the full path ahead. I will start each day this week by reading and meditating on a scripture passage."

Practice Exercise:

Write a short reflection on how your selected verse speaks to you personally. Include any actions you feel led to take as a result of this study.

Putting It All Together

Let's recap the process:

1. Select a Verse: Choose a verse that resonates with you.
2. Identify Keywords: Highlight significant words or phrases.
3. Explore Definitions: Dive into the original meanings of keywords.
4. Cross-Reference: Find related verses to broaden your understanding.
5. Apply Personally: Reflect on how the verse applies to your life.

Bible Verse Mapping transforms scripture study into an engaging and transformative experience. By breaking a verse into its components and reflecting on its meaning, you'll uncover the richness of God's Word and grow in your faith. In the next chapter, we'll explore how to create a visual map to organize and enhance your study. Keep going—you're on an exciting journey!

CHAPTER 5

Hands-On Example – Mapping Philippians 4:6

Now that we've covered the process of Bible Verse Mapping, let's put it into practice with a hands-on example. In this chapter, we'll map Philippians 4:6:

"Do not be anxious about anything, but in every situation, by prayer and petition, with thanksgiving, present your requests to God."

This verse is rich with meaning and practical application, making it an excellent choice for verse mapping. We'll walk through each step of the process, and by the end, you'll have a clear, visual map to reflect on and revisit.

Step 1: Select the Verse
We've already chosen Philippians 4:6 as our verse for this example. Take a moment to write it down in your journal or notebook, leaving space around it for notes, diagrams, and reflections.

Verse:
"Do not be anxious about anything, but in every situation, by prayer and petition, with thanksgiving, present your requests to God."

Why This Verse?
This verse speaks directly to the universal struggle with anxiety and offers practical guidance for turning to God in moments of worry. Its timeless relevance makes it a great verse to study.

Step 2: Identify Keywords
Next, we identify the keywords in the verse. Keywords are words or phrases central to its meaning. Here are the keywords for Philippians 4:6:

- **Anxious:** Highlights the emotional struggle addressed in the verse.
- **Anything:** Emphasizes the totality of God's invitation to trust Him with all concerns.
- **Prayer:** Indicates communication with God.
- **Petition:** Suggests specific, earnest requests.
- **Thanksgiving:** Focuses on gratitude in our relationship with God.
- **Requests:** Refers to our needs brought before God.

Write these keywords down in your journal, leaving space for definitions and related insights.

Step 3: Explore Definitions
To understand the depth of the keywords, let's explore their original Greek meanings using a concordance or Bible app:

- **Anxious (merimnaō):** To be divided, distracted, or pulled in different directions.
- **Prayer (proseuchē):** A general term for communicating with God, often encompassing worship and adoration.
- **Petition (deēsis):** A specific request or supplication, often with a sense of urgency

- **Thanksgiving (eucharistia):** Expressing gratitude and recognizing God's goodness.
- **Requests (aitēma):** Particular needs or desires brought before God.

Record these definitions in your journal, noting how they enrich your understanding of the verse.

Step 4: Cross-Reference
Now, find related verses to see how scripture supports and expands on this passage. Here are some cross-references for Philippians 4:6:

- **Matthew 6:25-34:** Jesus' teaching on not worrying, emphasizing God's provision.
- **1 Peter 5:7:** "Cast all your anxiety on him because he cares for you."
- **Colossians 4:2:** Encouragement to devote ourselves to prayer, being watchful and thankful.

Write these references in your journal, and note any key phrases or insights from the related verses. This step shows how the Bible's teachings on anxiety and prayer form a cohesive message.

Step 5: Personal Application
Reflect on what Philippians 4:6 means for your life. Ask yourself:

- What anxieties or worries do I need to surrender to God?
- How can I incorporate thanksgiving into my prayers?
- What does this verse teach me about trusting God?

Reflection Example:
"This verse reminds me that I don't need to carry my worries alone. God invites me to bring everything to Him in prayer, not just my big concerns but even the small things that weigh on my heart. By focusing on gratitude, I can shift my perspective from worry to trust."

Write down your personal reflections and consider how you'll apply this truth in your daily life.

Sample Map of Philippians 4:6
Here's an example of how your verse map might look:
Center of the Map:
- Write the verse in the center of your page:
- "Do not be anxious about anything, but in every situation, by prayer and petition, with thanksgiving, present your requests to God."

Keywords and Definitions:
- Around the verse, add the keywords and their definitions:
  - Anxious: Divided, distracted.
  - Prayer: Communication with God.
  - Petition: Specific requests.
  - Thanksgiving: Gratitude for God's goodness.
  - Requests: Particular needs.

Cross-References:
- Add related verses and a few words about their connection:
  - 1 Peter 5:7: "Cast all your anxiety on Him."
  - Matthew 6:25-34: God's care for His creation.
  - Colossians 4:2: Be thankful in prayer.

Personal Reflections:
- Add a section for your reflections and applications:
  - "I will make a habit of turning my worries into prayers, focusing on God's faithfulness."

Visual Elements:
- Use arrows to connect keywords to their definitions.
- Highlight the phrase "by prayer and petition, with thanksgiving" to emphasize the process of surrendering anxiety.
- Add color or symbols, like a lightbulb for insight or a heart for personal application.

Putting It All Together

Bible Verse Mapping transforms Philippians 4:6 from a verse you read to a truth you internalize. By exploring its keywords, definitions, cross-references, and applications, you gain a deeper understanding of its message and how it applies to your life.

This hands-on example is just the beginning. As you continue verse mapping, you'll uncover new insights, connect with God's Word in meaningful ways, and build a habit of intentional study. Now, it's your turn—pick a verse and start mapping!

CHAPTER 6

CREATING YOUR OWN VERSE MAP

Now that you've learned the steps of Bible Verse Mapping and practiced with Philippians 4:6, it's time to create your own map! This chapter will guide you through the process, provide templates to help you get started, and offer encouragement to make this a meaningful and enjoyable experience.

Step-by-Step Guide to Creating Your Verse Map

Follow this step-by-step guide to craft a verse map that reflects your personal journey with scripture. Remember, this process is flexible—feel free to adapt it to your style and preferences.

1. Choose Your Verse
Select a verse that resonates with you. Here are a few ideas to get you started:

- Psalm 23:1: "The Lord is my shepherd; I lack nothing."
- John 3:16: "For God so loved the world that he gave his one and only Son, that whoever believes in him shall not perish but have eternal life."
- Proverbs 3:5-6: "Trust in the Lord with all your heart and lean not on your own understanding; in all your ways submit to him, and he will make your paths straight."

Write the verse at the top or center of your page.

2. **Highlight Keywords**
 Underline, circle, or highlight the keywords in the verse. Look for words that are repeated, carry significant meaning, or stand out to you personally. Write these keywords around the verse, leaving space to add definitions and notes.

3. **Explore Definitions**
 Using a concordance or Bible app, look up the original Hebrew or Greek meanings of the keywords. Record their definitions, root words, and any nuances that deepen your understanding.

4. **Find Cross-References**
 Locate related verses that reinforce or expand on the verse's message. Write these references around the verse and note their key insights or connections.

5. **Add Personal Reflections**
Reflect on what the verse means for your life. Write your thoughts and applications in a dedicated section.
Consider questions like:
- How does this verse challenge or encourage me?
- What action is God calling me to take?
- How can I apply this truth to my daily life?

6. **Visualize Your Map**
Use lines, arrows, or color-coded sections to connect keywords, definitions, and cross-references. Add creative elements like doodles, symbols, or stickers to personalize your map.

Template for Your Verse Map
Here's a simple template you can use to organize your verse map:
Center of the Page: Write the verse in large, clear handwriting.

Section 1: Keywords
- List the keywords and leave space for their definitions.
- Example:
    - Trust: Complete reliance on God's character and promises.
    - Heart: Inner self, emotions, and intentions.

Section 2: Definitions
- Write the meanings of the keywords, including their original language and context.

Section 3: Cross-References
- List at least two related verses and their key insights.

Section 4: Reflections
- Write a short paragraph on how the verse speaks to your life.

Creative Elements
- Draw diagrams, use arrows to connect ideas, or add colors to highlight themes.

Encouragement for Your Journey

As you create your verse map, remember that this process is deeply personal. There's no right or wrong way to map scripture. Your map is a reflection of your unique walk with God, so don't worry about making it perfect. Focus on what you're learning and how God is speaking to you through His Word.

Here are a few tips to keep in mind:
- Start Small: Begin with short, familiar verses before moving on to longer passages.
- Be Patient: Give yourself time to grow comfortable with the process.
- Celebrate Progress: Each map is a step toward a deeper relationship with God.

Example Prompts for Practice

If you're unsure where to start, here are some verses to inspire your first maps:
- Psalm 46:10: "Be still, and know that I am God..."
- Isaiah 40:31: "But those who hope in the Lord will renew their strength..."
- Romans 8:28: "And we know that in all things God works for the good of those who love him..."

These verses offer rich opportunities for reflection and application.

A Personal Invitation

Bible Verse Mapping is a journey of discovery, reflection, and connection with God's Word. Each map you create is a record of how God has spoken to you, shaped your heart, and guided your steps. Over time, your journal will become a cherished collection of insights, prayers, and personal growth.

As you begin creating your own verse maps, remember to approach the process with joy and curiosity. Let God's Word speak to you in new and powerful ways. You're not just studying scripture—you're building a foundation for a deeper relationship with your Creator.

In the next chapter, we'll explore practical tips and tools to enhance your Bible Verse Mapping practice. Keep going—you're doing amazing work!

CHAPTER 7

Practical Tips and Tools

Bible Verse Mapping is a rewarding practice that helps you dive deeper into God's Word. To make the most of this method, it's important to equip yourself with the right tools, manage your time effectively, and develop a routine that fits your lifestyle. This chapter will provide you with practical tips and resources to enhance your verse mapping journey.

Tools for Bible Verse Mapping
Having the right tools can make the process smoother and more enjoyable. Here's a list of resources to help you get started and stay organized:

1. **Bible**
   - Use a version you're comfortable with, such as the NIV, ESV, or NLT.
   - A study Bible with footnotes and references can be especially helpful.
   - Access multiple translations to compare wording and gain deeper insight.

2. **Concordance**
   - A concordance is an invaluable tool for looking up keywords and their original Hebrew or Greek meanings.
   - Popular options include Strong's Concordance or online versions available through Bible apps and websites.

3. **Bible Apps**
   - Apps like Blue Letter Bible, Bible Gateway, and Logos Bible Software provide access to concordances, commentaries, and cross-references.
   - Many apps allow you to compare translations, explore word studies, and take notes.

4. **Notebook or Journal**
   - A dedicated notebook or journal is essential for recording your verse maps.
   - Consider using a dot-grid or blank notebook for flexibility in drawing diagrams and adding creative touches.

5. **Pens, Markers, and Highlighters**
   - Use colored pens and markers to highlight keywords, cross-references, and themes.
   - Color-coding adds a visual element that makes your maps easier to navigate.

6. **Additional Resources**
    - Commentaries: Books or online resources offering explanations and interpretations of scripture.
    - Lexicons: Tools that provide detailed meanings and contexts for Hebrew and Greek words.
    - Printable and Templates: Download verse mapping templates to keep your study organized

Time Management: Fitting Verse Mapping into Your Day
Life can be busy, but with intentional planning, you can incorporate Bible Verse Mapping into your daily routine. Here are some tips to help you make time for this enriching practice:

1. **Start Small**
    - Begin with 10-15 minutes a day. Focus on one step at a time rather than completing an entire map in one sitting.
    - For example, spend one day selecting a verse and identifying keywords, then explore definitions the next day.

2. **Set a Regular Time**
    - Choose a time of day when you're most alert and focused. Many people find mornings ideal for quiet study, while others prefer evenings for reflection.
    - Schedule your verse mapping session as a recurring part of your day, just like any other important appointment.
3. **Combine with Other Practices**
    - Pair verse mapping with your prayer or devotional time.
    - Use Sundays or weekends for extended mapping sessions to explore scripture more deeply.
4. **Be Flexible**
    - Some days might be busier than others. On those days, review an existing map instead of starting a new one.
    - Keep your tools handy so you can study during unexpected free moments.
5. **Create a Weekly Goal**
    - Aim to complete one or two verse maps each week. This pace allows for thorough study without feeling rushed.
6. **Stay Motivated**
    - Choose verses that excite and inspire you.
    - Mix up your approach by exploring different themes or focusing on favorite books of the Bible.

Practical Example: A Sample Routine
Here's an example of a simple weekly routine for verse mapping:
- Monday: Select a verse and write it in your journal.
- Tuesday: Highlight keywords and jot down initial observations.
- Wednesday: Look up definitions for two or three keywords.
- Thursday: Find and record two cross-references.
- Friday: Reflect on the verse and write a personal application.
- Saturday: Review your completed map and pray over the insights you've gained.

This routine breaks the process into manageable steps and ensures that each session is focused and meaningful.

Final Encouragement
Bible Verse Mapping is more than a study method—it's a spiritual practice that allows you to slow down, connect with God, and grow in understanding His Word. Remember, the goal isn't perfection but transformation. Each map reflects your journey, and every step brings you closer to God.

As you incorporate these tools, time management strategies, and routines into your study, you'll find verse mapping becoming a natural and enriching part of your life. In the next chapter, we'll explore how to use your verse maps for prayer, reflection, and deeper application. Keep going—you're doing fantastic work!

CHAPTER 8

SAMPLE VERSE MAPS

A picture is worth a thousand words, and in Bible Verse Mapping, seeing examples can inspire and guide your creative process. This chapter will explore a few sample verse maps and explain why specific keywords, definitions, cross-references, and reflections were included. Use these examples as inspiration to create your personalized maps.

Sample Verse Map 1: Psalm 23:1
Verse: "The Lord is my shepherd; I lack nothing."

1. **Keywords and Definitions**
   - Lord (Yahweh): The self-existing, covenant-keeping God.
   - Shepherd (ra'ah): One who tends, guides, and protects the flock.

Lack Nothing (lo' chaser): To have no deficiency or unmet needs

These keywords highlight God's character as a provider and protector, offering complete sufficiency to His people.

2. **Cross-References**
   - John 10:11: "I am the good shepherd. The good shepherd lays down his life for the sheep."
   - Ezekiel 34:11-12: God promises to search for and care for His sheep.

These references expand on the metaphor of God as a shepherd, emphasizing His care, guidance, and sacrificial love.

3. **Personal Reflections**

"This verse reassures me that I can trust God to provide everything I need, even in uncertain times. Like a shepherd, He knows what's best for me and leads me to what I truly need."

Illustration

In the center, the verse is written in bold letters. Surrounding it:
- Keywords are written in boxes with arrows leading to their definitions.
- Cross-references are listed on the left with lines connecting them to relevant keywords.
- At the bottom, a reflection is written in a curved shape, resembling a path, to symbolize the journey with God as our Shepherd.

Sample Verse Map 2: John 3:16

Verse: "For God so loved the world that he gave his one and only Son, that whoever believes in him shall not perish but have eternal life."

1. **Keywords and Definitions**
   - Loved (agapaō): An unconditional, selfless love.
   - World (kosmos): All humanity, emphasizing inclusivity.
   - Gave (didōmi): To freely offer or bestow.
   - Eternal Life (zōē aiōnios): A never-ending, God-infused quality of life.

These keywords focus on God's sacrificial love and the gift of salvation offered to everyone.

2. **Cross-References**
   - Romans 5:8: "But God demonstrates his love for us in this: While we were still sinners, Christ died for us."
   - 1 John 4:9: "This is how God showed his love among us: He sent his one and only Son into the world that we might live through him."

These references affirm God's immense love and initiative in offering salvation through Christ.

3. **Personal Reflections**

"This verse reminds me of the vastness of God's love for all people, including me. It challenges me to reflect this love in my relationships and fully trust His promise of eternal life."

Illustration

The verse is written in a heart shape in the center to represent love.

- Keywords are highlighted with different colors and connected with lines to their definitions.
- Cross-references are positioned around the heart, with arrows pointing to "Loved" and "Gave."
- The personal reflection is written in the margins as a "call to action."

Sample Verse Map 3: Proverbs 3:5-6

Verse: "Trust in the Lord with all your heart and lean not on your understanding; in all your ways submit to him, and he will make your paths straight."

1. **Keywords and Definitions**
   - Trust (batach): To have confidence, to rely on without fear.
   - Heart (leb): The inner self, including emotions, mind, and will.
   - Submit (yada): To know intimately; to acknowledge.
   - Paths Straight (yashar): To make smooth, direct, or right.

These keywords emphasize complete reliance on God intellectually, emotionally, and spiritually.

2. **Cross-References**
   - Psalm 37:5: "Commit your way to the Lord; trust in him and he will do this."
   - Isaiah 26:3: "You will keep in perfect peace those whose minds are steadfast because they trust in you."

These references reinforce trust and submission to God, leading to peace and direction.

3. **Personal Reflections**
"This verse reminds me to surrender my plans and worries to God. Trusting Him fully means letting go of control and believing He will guide me on the right path."

Illustration
The verse is written in the center with a winding path drawn beneath it to symbolize life's journey.
- Keywords are placed along the path with definitions written next to them.
- Cross-references are positioned like signposts on the path, connected by dotted lines.
- Personal reflections are written at the end of the path, symbolizing the destination of trust and submission.

Encouragement to Create Your Own
These sample verse maps show how flexible and creative Bible Verse Mapping can be. Use these examples as inspiration, but remember, your maps should reflect your insights and connection to scripture. Whether simple or elaborate, each map uniquely expresses your journey with God's Word. As you create your maps, focus on what resonates with you. Experiment with different layouts, colors, and styles until you find what works best. Most importantly, let the process draw you closer to God and deepen your understanding of His truth.

In the next chapter, we'll explore how to use your verse maps for prayer, reflection, and ongoing growth. Keep mapping—you're doing fantastic work!

CHAPTER 9

REFLECTIVE QUESTIONS AND EXERCISES

After completing a verse map, take time to think about its meaning and impact. Use the following questions to guide your reflection:

1. **Understanding the Verse**
   - What does this verse teach me about God's character?
   - How does the historical or cultural context shape my understanding of this verse?
   - What new insights did I gain from exploring the original Hebrew or Greek definitions?
2. **Connecting with Your Life**
   - How does this verse speak to my current season of life or the challenges I'm facing?

- Are there specific areas in my life where I need to trust or obey God more because of this verse?
- What does this verse teach me about my relationship with others?

3. **Applying the Truth**
   - How can I actively apply this verse to my daily routine, relationships, or decisions?
   - Is there a habit, thought pattern, or action I need to change based on this scripture?
   - How does this verse inspire me to grow spiritually or share my faith with others?

4. **Engaging in Prayer**
   - What do I want to thank God for after studying this verse?
   - Do I want to bring specific concerns or requests to God in light of this scripture?
   - How does this verse shape my understanding of approaching God in prayer?

Write down your responses in your journal or alongside your verse map. These reflections serve as a record of your spiritual growth and God's work in your life.

Practice Exercises: Strengthening Your Skills
Use these exercises to practice your mapping skills and enhance your ability to reflect on scripture.

1. Keyword Exploration Exercise
- Choose a verse you haven't mapped yet (e.g., Romans 12:2: "Do not conform to the pattern of this world but be transformed by the renewing of your mind.").
- Identify at least five keywords in the verse.
- Look up their definitions in a concordance or Bible app.
- Write a short paragraph summarizing how these keywords shape the meaning of the verse.

2. Cross-Referencing Challenge
- Select a verse you've already mapped.
- Find three additional cross-references that connect to the verse. Use a study Bible, concordance, or Bible app for guidance.
- Write a short note for each cross-reference explaining how it complements or reinforces the main verse.
- Example: For John 3:16, a related verse might be Romans 5:8: "But God demonstrates his love for us in this: While we were still sinners, Christ died for us." Write how this verse further highlights God's sacrificial love.

3. Personal Application Journal
- Choose one verse map you've completed recently.
- Write a journal entry answering the following:
  - How did this verse map deepen my understanding of the scripture?
  - What practical steps will I take this week to live out the truth of this verse?
  - How can I share the insights from this verse with someone else?

4. Create a Topical Map
- Pick a theme you want to explore, such as forgiveness, trust, or prayer.
- Choose three verses related to the theme and create a mini-map for each one.
- Compare the maps and write a summary of what you've learned about the theme.

Example:
- Theme: Trust
  - Proverbs 3:5-6
  - Psalm 56:3: "When I am afraid, I trust you."
  - Isaiah 26:3: "You will keep in perfect peace those whose minds are steadfast because they trust in you."

5. Map a Favorite Verse from Memory
- Select a verse you've memorized or one meaningful to you.
- Without looking it up, write the verse in your journal and try to map it from memory.

Afterward, check the verse in your Bible and compare your understanding. What did you recall accurately? What new insights did you gain from mapping it?

A Reflective Weekly Routine
To build consistency in your study, consider adopting a weekly routine for reflection and mapping. Here's a sample plan:
- **Day 1:** Select a verse and write it down.
- **Day 2:** Highlight keywords and look up their definitions.
- **Day 3:** Find and record cross-references.
- **Day 4:** Write a reflection or journal entry about the verse.
- **Day 5:** Create a prayer inspired by the verse.
- **Day 6:** Review your map and share it with a friend, family member, or study group.
- **Day 7:** Revisit past maps and reflect on how they've shaped your faith journey.

Final Encouragement
Reflection and application transform Bible Verse Mapping from a study tool into a life-changing spiritual discipline. Consider deeply what you've learned and invite God to use His Word to shape your thoughts, attitudes, and actions.

Remember, each map you create is a step closer to understanding God's heart and purpose for your life. The more you reflect, the more you'll grow in faith, knowledge, and love for God's Word.

In the next chapter, we'll explore how to use your verse maps for prayer, group study, and other practical applications. Keep reflecting, practicing, and mapping—you're building a solid foundation for a lifetime of spiritual growth!

CHAPTER 10

MOVING FORWARD – DEVELOPING A VERSE MAPPING PRACTICE

Bible Verse Mapping is more than a one-time study tool—it's a spiritual habit that can deepen your understanding of God's Word over time. This chapter will guide you in establishing a sustainable verse mapping practice, encouraging collaboration with others, and incorporating your maps into prayer and reflection for a more prosperous devotional life.

Creating a Routine: Strategies for Consistent Study

Developing a routine is vital to making Bible Verse Mapping a regular part of your life. Here are some strategies to help you stay consistent:

1. **Start Small**
   - Begin with one verse map per week. This manageable goal prevents you from being overwhelmed and gives you time to reflect deeply on each verse.
   - As mapping becomes more familiar, you can increase the frequency or explore multiple verses around a specific theme.

2. **Set a Dedicated Time**
   - Choose a time of day when you can focus without distractions. Many people find mornings or evenings ideal for uninterrupted study.
   - Block off this time on your calendar to treat it as an essential appointment.

3. **Plan Ahead**
   - At the beginning of each week, decide which verse(s) you'll map. This preparation saves time and keeps you focused.
   - If you're following a Bible reading plan or sermon series, align your verse maps with those topics for a cohesive study experience.

4. **Mix It Up**
   - Alternate between individual verses and themes (e.g., hope, forgiveness, trust) to keep your study fresh.
   - Incorporate seasonal scriptures, such as Advent verses during Christmas or resurrection themes during Easter.

5. Track Your Progress
- Use a journal or planner to record your mapped verses and reflect on your learning.
- Celebrate milestones, such as completing 10 verse maps or a thematic series, to stay motivated.

Finding a Study Partner: Sharing Insights with Others
While verse mapping is a personal practice, sharing your insights with others can enhance and encourage your learning. Here's how collaboration can enrich your experience:

1. Study Together
- Partner with a friend or family member to map the same verse and compare your findings. This shared study can reveal perspectives you may not have considered.
- Join or start a Bible study group where verse mapping is a regular activity. Group discussions can provide valuable context and foster deeper connections.

2. Encourage Accountability
- Having a study partner can help you stay consistent. Check-in with each other weekly to share your progress and insights.
- Set shared goals, such as completing a series of maps on a particular book of the Bible, and celebrate your achievements together.

3. Share Completed Maps
- Use your completed maps as conversation starters or teaching tools. Sharing your reflections can inspire others and create opportunities for meaningful dialogue about scripture.
- Consider hosting a small group session where everyone presents their favorite verse map and discusses its impact.

Using Maps for Prayer and Reflection

Completed verse maps are more than study tools—they're potent resources for prayer and meditation. Here are some ways to incorporate them into your devotional life:

1. Turn Your Maps into Prayers
- Use the insights from your verse map to shape your prayers. For example, if you mapped Philippians 4:6 ("Do not be anxious about anything..."), pray for peace and gratitude in your current circumstances.
- Personalize your prayer by incorporating your map's keywords, reflections, and cross-references.

2. Meditate on Key Truths
- Revisit your completed maps during quiet time, focusing on your recorded truths and applications.
- Use your map to guide scripture meditation, letting the verse and its meaning resonate in your heart and mind.

3. Create a Gratitude Journal
- Use your maps to reflect on God's goodness and faithfulness. Write down moments in your life where the verse's truths were evident.
- For example, if you mapped Psalm 23:1 ("The Lord is my shepherd..."), journal instances where God provided guidance or comfort.

4. Use Maps in Worship
- Share a verse map with your church small group, youth ministry, or family devotionals. Use it as a foundation for group prayer or worship sessions.
- Let the truths from your verse map inspire praise and thanksgiving during personal or corporate worship.

Sustaining Your Practice

As you move forward, remember that Bible Verse Mapping is a flexible and evolving practice. It's not about perfection but connecting with God's Word meaningfully. Here are some final tips to keep your practice sustainable:
- Be Patient with Yourself: Some verses might take longer to map than others, and that's okay. Give yourself the grace to grow at your own pace.
- Adapt to Your Season: Life changes, and so can your practice. During busy seasons, simplify your mapping process or revisit old maps instead of starting new ones.
- Stay Inspired: Regularly explore new themes, verses, or creative approaches to mapping to keep your study engaging

CHAPTER 11

Resources and Recommended Readings

The right tools and resources make building a rich Bible study practice easier. This chapter provides a curated list of apps, books, and online communities to support your journey in Bible Verse Mapping. Whether you're looking for study tools, inspiration, or a place to share your insights, you'll find something here to enhance your experience.

Bible Study Tools
Having reliable tools at your fingertips can make verse mapping more effective and enjoyable. Here are some must-have resources:

1. Bible Apps and Websites
 These apps provide easy access to Bible translations, concordances, and commentaries. Most are free or offer premium features.
- Blue Letter Bible
- A comprehensive app for exploring the original Hebrew and Greek, cross-references, and commentaries.

- Website: blueletterbible.org
- Bible Gateway
- Offers multiple translations, reading plans, and study notes. Premium versions include access to commentaries and lexicons.
- Website: biblegateway.com
- Logos Bible Software
- A powerful tool for in-depth study with extensive libraries, interactive maps, and advanced search features. Free and paid options are available.
- Website: logos.com
- YouVersion Bible App
- Perfect for on-the-go access to Bible translations, daily devotionals, and verse-of-the-day features.
- Website: youversion.com

2. Concordances

Concordances are invaluable for exploring original language meanings and locating verses. Here are a few trusted options:

Strong's Exhaustive Concordance

A classic resource for word studies, linking every English word in the Bible to its original Hebrew or Greek term.

Vine's Expository Dictionary of Old and New Testament Words

Explains the meaning and usage of words in their biblical context.

Nave's Topical Bible

Arrange verses by topic, making exploring themes like forgiveness, love, or trust easy.

3. Study Bibles

Study Bibles include helpful notes, maps, and cross-references. Some excellent choices include:
- ESV Study Bible
- Known for its scholarly notes and theological insights.
- NIV Life Application Study Bible
- Focuses on practical applications for daily life.
- The MacArthur Study Bible
- Offers detailed verse-by-verse commentary.
- The Message Study Bible
- Includes contemporary language and reflection prompts, ideal for personal devotion.

Recommended Books

Books on Bible study and personal growth can inspire and deepen your understanding of scripture. Here are some standout titles:

1. Books on Bible Study Techniques
   - "How to Read the Bible for All Its Worth" by Gordon D. Fee and Douglas Stuart
   - A guide to interpreting scripture responsibly and effectively.
   - "Living by the Book" by Howard G. Hendricks and William D. Hendricks
   - A practical book for studying and applying the Bible in daily life.
   - "Grasping God's Word" by J. Scott Duvall and J. Daniel Hays

Offers a hands-on approach to understanding scripture in its context.

2. Books on Spiritual Growth

"Celebration of Discipline" by Richard J. Foster
Explores spiritual disciplines, including Bible study, prayer, and meditation.

"The Purpose Driven Life" by Rick Warren
It helps readers discover their purpose through scripture.

"Women of the Word" by Jen Wilkin
Teaches how to approach Bible study with intentionality and focus.

3. Devotional Books

"Jesus Calling" by Sarah Young
A daily devotional with scripture-based reflections.

"My Utmost for His Highest" by Oswald Chambers
It is a timeless classic offering deep spiritual insights.

Websites and Online Communities

Connect with other Bible students and find inspiration through these websites and communities:

1. Online Communities for Bible Study

The Bible Project
Provides videos, podcasts, and articles explaining biblical themes and books.
Website: bibleproject.com

She Reads Truth/He Reads Truth
Communities focused on daily Bible reading plans and devotionals.

Website: shereadstruth.com
YouVersion Community
Participate in Bible reading challenges and interact with others through shared plans.

2. Blogs and Articles
Desiring God
Articles, podcasts, and resources focusing on scripture and theology.
Website: desiringgod.org
Bible Study Tools
Offers articles, devotionals, and study aids for deeper engagement with scripture.
Website: biblestudytools.com

3. Social Media Groups
Search for Bible study groups on platforms like Facebook or Instagram. Many communities share verse mapping tips, completed maps, and encouragement.

Using These Resources Effectively

With so many tools and resources available, choosing what works best for your needs and goals is essential. Start with a few basic tools, such as a Bible app and a concordance, and gradually add more as your study deepens. Explore recommended books and communities for additional inspiration and support.

A Final Note

Equipping yourself with the right resources is an investment in your spiritual growth. These tools, books, and communities enhance your understanding of scripture and encourage you to engage with God's Word meaningfully.

As you continue your verse mapping journey, remember that the ultimate resource is the Holy Spirit, who guides and illuminates the truth of God's Word. Seek His wisdom, and let these tools support your walk with Him.

In the final chapter, we'll conclude with encouragement and a vision for how Bible Verse Mapping can continue to shape your faith journey. Keep exploring and growing—you're building a foundation for a lifetime of study and devotion!

CHAPTER 12

CONCLUSION

Congratulations! You've completed this journey into Bible Verse Mapping. Whether you're just beginning to explore this method or have already started creating your maps, you've taken meaningful steps toward a deeper understanding of God's Word and a more prosperous relationship with Him. In this final chapter, we'll celebrate your progress, discuss the next steps, and reflect on the eternal value of connecting with scripture.

Encouragement: Celebrating Your Progress

Take a moment to reflect on all you've accomplished. You've learned to break down scripture into meaningful parts, explore original language definitions, find cross-references, and apply

God's truth to your life. You've created verse maps that are uniquely yours, representing your growth in faith and understanding.

Your effort in this journey is worth celebrating because it's not just about learning—it's about transformation. Every map you've created, every keyword you've defined, and every reflection you've written is a testament to your desire to know God more deeply. That is something to rejoice in!
Remember that growth in understanding scripture is a lifelong process. Each step brings you closer to God, and He delights in your desire to know Him through His Word.

Next Steps: Continuing Your Journey
Bible Verse Mapping is not just a study method; it's a spiritual practice you can carry with you for the rest of your life. Here are some next steps to help you continue growing:

1. Create a Verse Mapping Routine
- Commit to a regular time for mapping, whether daily, weekly, or monthly.
- Set goals, such as mapping a specific number of verses or studying a particular theme, like grace, prayer, or trust.

2. Explore Different Themes and Books of the Bible
- Use verse mapping to dive into a book of the Bible, such as Psalms, Proverbs, or John.
- Focus on themes that resonate with your current life season, such as peace during challenging times or hope in a season of waiting.

3. Share Your Maps with Others
- Start a small group or study partner arrangement where you can share insights from your verse maps.
- Use your maps as a teaching tool for friends, family, or church members interested in learning more about scripture.

4. Revisit Your Completed Maps
- Go back to maps you've created in the past and reflect on how God has worked in your life since you studied those verses.
- Update or expand your maps with new insights as your understanding grows.

5. Pray Over Your Maps
- Use your completed maps as a guide for prayer. Thank God for what He's revealed, and ask Him to help you live out the truths you've studied

Final Reflection: The Eternal Value of Connecting with God's Word

Bible Verse Mapping is about more than learning facts or completing a study. It's about meeting God in His Word, hearing His voice, and allowing His truth to transform your heart and life. The more you engage with scripture, the more you see its relevance in your daily decisions, relationships, and spiritual growth.
In Hebrews 4:12, we're reminded that "the word of God is alive and active. Sharper than any double-edged sword, it penetrates even to dividing soul and spirit, joints and marrow; it judges the thoughts and attitudes of the heart." When you take the time to map God's Word, you're allowing His living truth to shape you in ways that go beyond what you can imagine.

As you move forward, let Bible Verse Mapping be a tool that deepens your understanding of God's love, strengthens your faith, and equips you to share His truth with others. Each verse you map is another opportunity to draw closer to the Creator, who knows and loves you more than anyone else.

A Closing Prayer

Let's end this journey with a prayer:

Heavenly Father,
Thank You for the gift of Your Word, a lamp to our feet and a light to our path. Thank You for the insights You've given us as we've explored scripture through Bible Verse Mapping. May the truths we've studied take root in our hearts and transform our lives. Help us continue seeking You through Your Word, growing in understanding, and living out Your truth daily. Bless every reader on this journey and guide them as they deepen their relationship with You. In Jesus' name, Amen.

Your Journey Continues
This may be the final chapter of this book, but your journey with Bible Verse Mapping is just beginning. Keep exploring, reflecting, and connecting with God through His Word. You'll discover new depths of His wisdom, love, and purpose for your life as you do. You're equipped with the tools and skills to engage with scripture powerfully. Go confidently, knowing God's Word is always there to guide, comfort, and inspire you. Happy mapping!

Appendices

The appendices provide practical tools and resources to help you continue your Bible Verse Mapping journey.

Here, you'll find a completed verse map example, a blank template for your use, a list of suggested verses for further practice, and a glossary of **Bible study terms.**

1. Sample Completed Verse Map

Verse: Proverbs 3:5-6

"Trust in the Lord with all your heart and lean not on your understanding; in all your ways submit to him, and he will make your paths straight."

Keywords and Definitions

- Trust (batach): To rely on with confidence; a sense of security.
- Heart (leb): The center of emotions, will, and understanding.
- Understanding (Binah): Insight or discernment from human reasoning.
- Submit (yada): To acknowledge or know intimately.
- Paths Straight (yashar): To make smooth, direct, or upright.

Cross-References

- Psalm 37:5: "Commit your way to the Lord; trust in him and he will do this."
- Isaiah 26:3: "You will keep in perfect peace those whose minds are steadfast because they trust in you."

Personal Reflections

"This verse reminds me that trusting God means surrendering control, even when things don't make sense. I must acknowledge His wisdom and guidance in all areas of my life. I can confidently walk forward when I do, knowing He will direct my steps."

Illustration
- The verse is written in the center with keywords in separate circles.
- Definitions and cross-references are connected to the keywords with arrows.
- A winding path at the bottom of the map symbolizes life's journey, leading to the words "God's Guidance."

2. Blank Template for Verse Mapping

Use the following template to guide your study. Please print it out or copy it into your journal.

Verse Mapping Template
1. Verse
Write the verse here:

2. Keywords
Highlight and list critical words or phrases from the verse:

_____
_____
_____
_____
_____
_____
_____

3. Definitions
Look up the original meanings of keywords in Hebrew or Greek. Write the definitions here:

_____
_____
_____
_____
_____
_____
_____

4. Cross-References
Find related scriptures that connect to this verse:

5. Reflections
What does this verse teach me? How can I apply it to my life?

6. Visual Elements (Optional)
Draw connections, use colors, or add diagrams to represent your insights.

3. Additional Verses for Practice
Here are some suggested verses to explore with the verse mapping method:

Trust and Guidance
- Psalm 23:1: "The Lord is my shepherd; I lack nothing."
- Isaiah 41:10: "So do not fear, for I am with you..."

Love and Forgiveness
- 1 Corinthians 13:4-7: "Love is patient, love is kind..."
- Ephesians 4:32: "Be kind and compassionate to one another..."

4. Glossary of Bible Study Terms

This glossary explains standard terms used in Bible study to enhance your understanding.

- Concordance: A tool that lists words from the Bible and where they occur, often including their original language meanings.
- Cross-Reference: A verse or passage that relates to another, providing additional context or insight.
- Commentary: An explanation or interpretation of scripture by biblical scholars.
- Hebrew/Greek Study: Analyzing the original languages of the Bible to uncover the whole meaning of words and phrases.
- Lexicon: A dictionary that defines Hebrew or Greek words used in the Bible.
- Meditation: Reflecting deeply on a verse or passage to understand its meaning and apply it to your life.
- Paraphrase: A restatement of a Bible verse in more straightforward or contemporary language for clarity.
- Scripture Context: Understanding a passage's surrounding verses, historical setting, and purpose.
- Study Bible: A Bible with additional notes, maps, and tools to assist with study and interpretation.

Thematic Study: Focusing on a specific theme (e.g., forgiveness, faith) by exploring related verses throughout the Bible

Final Note

These appendices equip you with practical tools and inspiration for your verse-mapping journey. Use the templates, explore the suggested verses, and refer to the glossary as you grow in your understanding of scripture. Happy mapping!

Verse Mapping Template
1. Verse
Write the verse here:

2. Keywords
Highlight and list critical words or phrases from the verse:

_____
_____
_____
_____
_____
_____
_____

3. Definitions
Look up the original meanings of keywords in Hebrew or Greek. Write the definitions here:

_____
_____
_____
_____
_____
_____
_____

4. Cross-References
Find related scriptures that connect to this verse:

_____
_____
_____
_____
_____
_____
_____

5. Reflections
What does this verse teach me? How can I apply it to my life?

_____
_____
_____
_____
_____
_____
_____

6. Visual Elements (Optional)

Draw connections, use colors, or add diagrams to represent your insights.

Verse Mapping Template
1. Verse
Write the verse here:

2. Keywords
Highlight and list critical words or phrases from the verse:

3. Definitions
Look up the original meanings of keywords in Hebrew or Greek. Write the definitions here:

4. Cross-References
Find related scriptures that connect to this verse:

_____
_____
_____
_____
_____
_____
_____

5. Reflections
What does this verse teach me? How can I apply it to my life?

_____
_____
_____
_____
_____
_____
_____

6. Visual Elements (Optional)
Draw connections, use colors, or add diagrams to represent your insights.

Verse Mapping Template
1. Verse
Write the verse here:

2. Keywords
Highlight and list critical words or phrases from the verse:

_____
_____
_____
_____
_____
_____
_____

3. Definitions
Look up the original meanings of keywords in Hebrew or Greek. Write the definitions here:

_____
_____
_____
_____
_____
_____
_____

4. Cross-References
Find related scriptures that connect to this verse:

5. Reflections
What does this verse teach me? How can I apply it to my life?

6. Visual Elements (Optional)

Draw connections, use colors, or add diagrams to represent your insights.

ABOUT THE AUTHOR

I am passionate about spreading the Gospel of Jesus Christ through Christian Education. With over 15 years of teaching experience, God has gifted me the ability to simplify complex principles and make them accessible to others. My personal journey of understanding the Bible and preachers' messages has shaped my teaching approach. I have experienced firsthand how God reveals His truth through dreams and visions, which has deepened my understanding of His word. In addition to my teaching ministry, I have been actively involved in church leadership for over two decades. Although I initially desired a more behind-the-scenes role, God redirected me to share His message actively. My educational background includes an associate's degree in early childhood education, a bachelor's degree in Birth-Kindergarten, and a master's degree in Birth-Kindergarten. I have also obtained certificates in community college instruction and autism and autism spectrum disorders. I hold a Doctoral degree in Christian Leadership, furthering my knowledge and expertise in this field.